CONTENTS

Published 2023.
Little Brother Books Ltd, Ground Floor, 23 Southernhay East, Exeter, Devon, EX1 1QL
Printed in China. EU address: Korte Leemstraat 3, 2018 Antwerpen, Belgium
books@littlebrotherbooks.co.uk | www.littlebrotherbooks.co.uk
The Little Brother Books trademarks, logos, email and website addresses, and the
GamesWarrior logo and imprint are sole and exclusive properties of Little Brother Books Limited.

ENTER THE EPIC WORLD OF...
MARIO & ‹‹‹‹‹‹
NINTENDO

Mario, Luigi, Bowser, Donkey Kong, Princess Peach, Toad... the cool characters from the Super Mario world are vast and exciting! When they're joined by loads more famous Nintendo stars, such as Pikachu, Link and Sonic, then it's the greatest gang of computer legends. A total gamer's paradise!

This *Ultimate Guide to Mario and Nintendo* reveals all you need to know about these iconic heroes and the biggest games of all time. You'll discover fun facts, strange stuff and mega Mario world news. Check out the most awesome action from the Mushroom Kingdom and beyond, plus a look at the most thrilling Nintendo titles over the years.

IF YOU LOVE MARIO AND NINTENDO, THEN THIS IS AN ADVENTURE YOU CAN'T MISS. LOAD UP AND ENJOY!

MEGA MARIO

There are over 300 Mario and Mario themed spin-off video games in total!

MEET MARIO

How much do you know about the adventurous hero and his rise to computer superstar?

BROTHER BOTHER

Mario's battles alongside his brother Luigi are legendary. Decked in overalls and a green top and cap, Luigi is much like his bro but not quite as brave. Together the pair take on lots of missions – thankfully they always come out on top!

DONKEY DEBUT

Mario actually has Donkey Kong, his long-time rival and occasional helper, to thank for his stardom! An arcade amusement game featuring DK was released in 1981. Mario was just a new side character in the game back then.

JOB LOT

Everyone knows Mario is a plumber, but he was originally described as a carpenter for the *Donkey Kong* arcade game in the '80s. Over the years he's had lots of jobs, from doctor to builder, golfer, tennis player, racing driver and artist. Mario is definitely multi-talented!

MUSHROOM MAYHEM

Mario lives in the mighty Mushroom Kingdom. Princess Peach rules this magical place, but whenever she gets troubled by Bowser (which happens a lot!) then Mario and his mates are ready to strike back. The Mushroom Kingdom sounds idyllic, but it has dangers and pitfalls!

AWESOME POWERS

Is there anything this Nintendo warrior can't do? Well, with slick speed, colossal jumping, huge strength, amazing durability and fancy footwork, Mario has the powers to beat opponents and find a route to victory. He's much more than just a likeable plumber.

VITAL ITEMS

Picking up special items keeps Mario in his best shape. Mushrooms give a brilliant boost to his size, feathers deliver agility and jumping, shells can be blasted at opponents and fire flowers create chaotic flame balls. All these power-ups are crucial for Mario's success!

DID YOU KNOW?

Mario got his name because the Nintendo bosses thought he looked like a person at their New York office called Mario Segali!

7

BACK IN TIME

Take a rapid ride through the years to see Mario's amazing journey. Hold on tight!

1981

Mario pops up for the first time, as part of the *Donkey Kong* coin-operated arcade machine. His character is actually known as Jumpman!

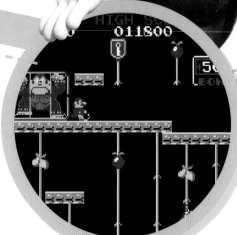

1991

The *Super Mario World* game on the Super Nintendo Entertainment System (SNES) console sees Yoshi, the loveable dinosaur, appear as Mario's mate!

1992

In one of the greatest adventures for Mario and his pals, gamers get behind the wheel for the first time in *Super Mario Kart!*

1996

It's the launch of the futuristic Nintendo 64 machine, the world's first realistic 3D home console. *Super Mario 64* is the must-have game!

1983

Now called Mario and not Jumpman, the hero appears in some small handheld Nintendo games called Game & Watch, along with other characters.

1985

Mario breaks out for his debut computer console adventure! Along with Luigi, they team up in *Super Mario Bros.* on the Nintendo Entertainment System (NES).

1988

Super Mario Bros. sells millions and is mega popular. Three years later, *Super Mario Bros. 2* hits the shops. Fans are mad for Mario!

1990

Mario is now a sky-high videogame character, because in *Super Mario Bros. 3* he flies for the first time! Bowser and his seven naughty children must be stopped!

2000

Mario Tennis is another 'ace' game on the N64. Nintendo fans are really seeing the sporty side of their energetic computer hero!

1999

Mario is one of the original characters in Nintendo's fun fighting game *Super Smash Bros.*, out this year. Bosh!

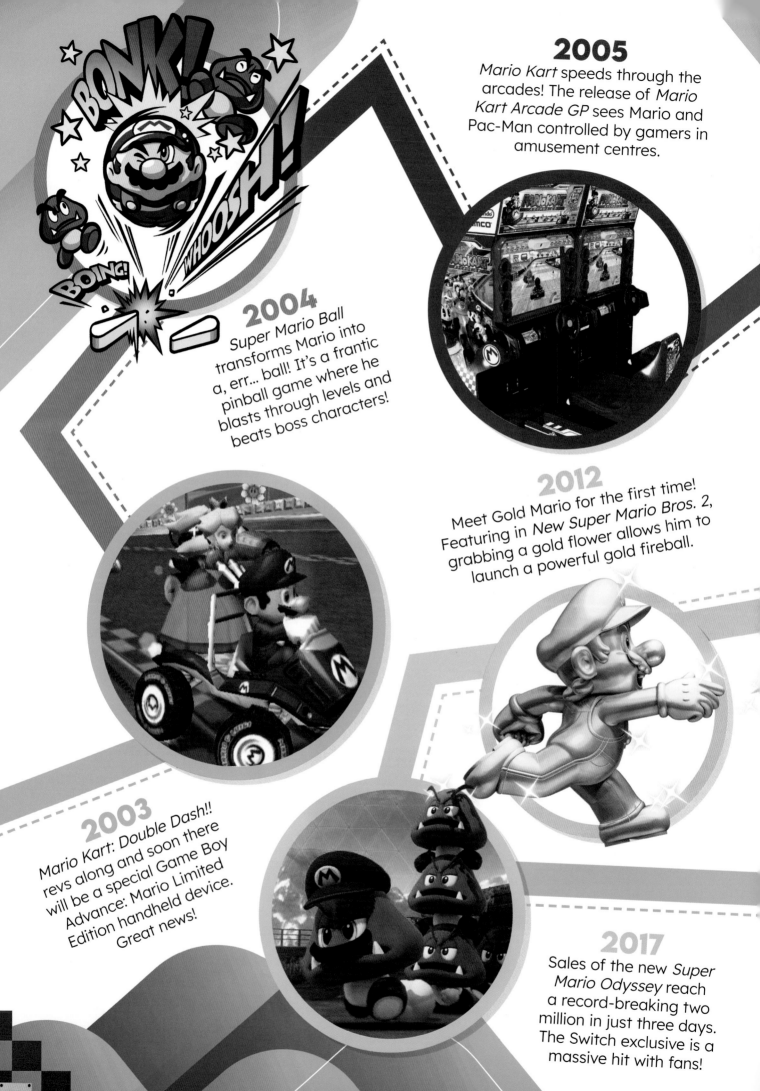

2005

Mario Kart speeds through the arcades! The release of *Mario Kart Arcade GP* sees Mario and Pac-Man controlled by gamers in amusement centres.

2004

Super Mario Ball transforms Mario into a, err... ball! It's a frantic pinball game where he blasts through levels and beats boss characters!

2012

Meet Gold Mario for the first time! Featuring in *New Super Mario Bros. 2*, grabbing a gold flower allows him to launch a powerful gold fireball.

2003

Mario Kart: Double Dash!! revs along and soon there will be a special Game Boy Advance: Mario Limited Edition handheld device. Great news!

2017

Sales of the new *Super Mario Odyssey* reach a record-breaking two million in just three days. The Switch exclusive is a massive hit with fans!

2006

In a huge new twist, this time Mario needs rescuing by Princess Peach! The Mushroom Kingdom ruler leads the way in the *Super Princess Peach* game.

2008

Mario partners with Sonic for the first time. The heroic pair prepare for a multi-sport blitz in *Mario & Sonic at the Olympic Games!*

2008

The Walk of Game is a new honour in Hollywood, where the world's gaming stars are recognised along a glitzy path. Mario is the first to get the prize!

WALK OF GAME

2023

The Super Nintendo World attraction opens in Hollywood. It's the ultimate place to worship Mario and you can even have a VR kart race with Bowser!

2023

Film fans can catch the brill *Super Mario Bros. Movie!* All the big Mushroom Kingdom characters take to the screen in this thrilling Nintendo adventure.

LUIGI ♥

#1

> Mario's biggest and best friend has got to be his bro, Luigi. Let's look at the exciting life and times of this gaming great!

FAMILY FUN

Since 1983, Luigi and Mario have been a top team, taking on Bowser, Koopa Troopas and many more enemies! Once he gets over his nerves in a battle, Luigi can actually jump higher than his bro and he unleashes all of the same powers. They appear very similar, but take a close-up look and you'll notice he's taller than Mario. Together they make a great double act!

TRAPPED!
In *Luigi's Mansion*, the unlucky Mario is trapped inside an old painting!

GHOSTLY FRIGHT

Luigi's first frightening fight with ghosts was in the *Luigi's Mansion* game. He enters a haunted home that's packed with creepy creatures and using his special Poltergust 3000 vacuum cleaner, Luigi tries to suck them all up. The King Boo ghost becomes Luigi's ultimate enemy!

GO, GO GOOIGI!

Professor E. Gadd, Luigi's ally, invents a special slimy version of Luigi called Gooigi! It's a gooey clone that has also mastered the Poltergust machine and helps rid the mansion of unwanted beings. It is easy to identify and even has a 'G' on its cap instead of 'L'

LUIGI PARTY

In 2013, Nintendo celebrated Luigi's 30th year as a videogame megastar and made it the Year of Luigi! New games released included *Luigi's Mansion 2, Mario & Luigi: Dream Team Bros. and New Super Luigi U.* The green superstar didn't really like being in the spotlight and couldn't wait for the celebrations to stop!

3 FUN FACTS

1 Luigi is Mario's twin, but Mario was born first!

2 Luigi's moustache is actually different to Mario's!

3 Luigi braves nasty viruses in the Dr. Luigi game!

BACK IN TIME

Did you know Luigi and Mario can time travel? In the *Partners in Time* game, they travel back and meet their younger selves, taking on mushroom alien Shroobs to save Princess Peach! The baby brothers join in with the grown-up brothers – it's an awesome foursome and so much fun!

SECRET MOVES

Give Luigi a super-sized swing playing in *Mario Golf: Super Rush* on the Switch. Luigi's special move is his incredible ice flower freeze and don't forget to use his power-packed speed-skate dash to zoom through the course. Keeping on a par with Luigi's golfing greatness isn't easy!

#2 PRINCESS PEACH

+

The number one lady in Mario's life is this famous royal. Find out what makes Peach a popular part of the Mario universe!

CASTLE CRUSADE

She lives in the Mushroom Kingdom, inside Peach's Castle. Its rooms seem to be endless and there are adventures and tests along its creepy corridors and lurking behind every door. Peach's Castle has the racetrack wrapped around it in *Mario Kart 8* and in the *Paper Mario* game, Peach's home is engulfed by Bowser's Castle!

POPULAR PRINCESS

No other female character has appeared in as many videogames as Princess Peach. By 2023, the powerful pink royal had been in more than 90 titles! Peach and Mario have a close bond and it's easy to see why – he's rescued her from Bowser hundreds of times over the years.

GOOD VIBES

In the *Super Princess Peach* game, she encounters Bowser's mystical Vibe Island and uses her magical emotions to track down Mario and Luigi. Her joy emotion can be used as both a weapon and a power-up and her rage move burns through opponents. Peach looks like a quiet and peaceful princess, but don't ignore her all-conquering abilities!

SUIT SWITCH

Peach rocks her royal robes most of the time, but in *Mario Kart* look out for her racing suit when she's on bikes and all-terrain vehicles. She also has an unlockable version called Pink Gold Peach. Win a grand prix and this glitzy girl could make an appearance on the track!

FIGHTING FORCE

The adventurous Peach has also appeared in Nintendo's *The Legend of Zelda* and *Super Smash Bros.* series of games. The Princess can be a fierce force – in *Smash Bros.* keep an eye on her evasive leaps into the air using her parasol. In *Paper Mario* the parasol lets her create a special disguise!

3 FUN FACTS

1 Her full name is Princess Peach Toadstool!

2 She enjoys baking and cooking – Mario likes that!

3 Her parents are the Mushroom King and Mushroom Queen.

ROYAL PARDON

Nintendo's *Tower Princess* game in 2022 had a pink princess, but it wasn't Peach!

MARIO'S TOP 10 FRIENDS...

#3 TOAD

>>>

Every Mario gamer gets a buzz when cheerful Toad takes on a challenge. Spend a little time getting to know the mini marvel!

TOAD TAKEOVER

Mario Kart, Super Mario Bros., Mario & Sonic – Toad pops up in all of these awesome adventures and loads more! A loyal servant to Princess Peach, he likes to keep a big smile on his little face, even when the Koopa Troop are causing destruction in the Kingdom!

RACE READY
You can cruise through Toad Harbor and Toad's Turnpike courses in *Mario Kart 8*!

COLOUR CLASH

Toad is easy to spot as he whizzes past in a kart. Although he's a tiny character, his big mushroom head stands out with its red dots. There are also blue and yellow dotted versions throughout the Mario world, but it's the red and white-headed Toad that fans love being in charge of.

CAPTAIN CALLING

In 2015 Toad's name was finally used in a game title – *Captain Toad Treasure Tracker* is such a blast! This is a cool puzzle platform, giving Nintendo fans the chance to really put Toad to the test as he tackles volcanoes, dragons and haunted houses. Scary!

3 FUN FACTS

1 He does Super Toad Dives in Mario Tennis Aces!

2 Toadette is Toad's top female friend!

3 He is sometimes called Toadsworth!

MINECRAFT MASH-UP

Because Toad is a computer legend, he is part of the exclusive Super Mario Mash-Up Pack where Nintendo faves get to appear in Minecraft. Toad's skin looks awesome in the block-based game, alongside Mario, Luigi and Princess Peach. He's more than a match for Minecraft Bowser!

SPEEDY STAR

Toad is best known for his lightning-fast drives in *Mario Kart*. Being small and lightweight means he has epic acceleration and mixed with his swerve and drift skills he is a proper force on karting circuits. But reaching high top speeds is not easy for Toad!

BACK-UP BRIGADE

Don't worry – the official Toad army is coming to the rescue! A group of helpful Toads, known as Toad Brigade, are always willing to help the good team in Mario games. They join the action in *Super Mario Odyssey*, *Super Mario Galaxy* and *Super Mario 3D World*. Get to it, gang!

#4 YOSHI

Get more creature comforts with a close-up look at Yoshi! He is always a helpful hero in Super Mario adventures.

MEGA MOUTH

In a showdown with Bowser and the Mushroom Kingdom's top enemies, Yoshi has some special powers. He can lash out his tongue to snap up fruit and foes, creating eggs with them which can then be thrown at targets. Yoshi's mouth is a potent weapon!

DINO DETAILS

Coming from Yoshi Island, this cute green dinosaur-like dude will do anything to help his mates! Yoshi is one of the Super Mario old skool heroes and first showed up in 1990's Super Mario World. Recently he's appeared in *Mario Strikers: Battle League*, *Mario & Rabbids Sparks of Hope* and *Super Mario Odyssey*. What a gaming great!

FLUTTER JUMPS

Yoshi was the first to master the flutter jump move, a tactic other heroes have also used in Super Mario games. A flutter jump is done by frantically flapping arms and legs, keeping Yoshi in the air and helping him reach high places his friends can't get to. Yoshi always fancies a quick flutter.

3 FUN FACTS

1 Yoshi has the power to become Super Yoshi!

2 Yoshi can give friends a ride on his back!

3 Yoshi is much taller than Mario!

SOFT TARGET

Because Yoshi is so soft and lovable, Nintendo has also made him a woolly creature! *Yoshi's Woolly World* and *Yoshi's Crafted World* are two games where he's made of soft material and the universe is a mix of wool, yarn, cloth and textiles. It's weird, but Yoshi is sooo cute and cuddly!

EGG-CELLENT!

Yoshi's New Island is a favourite game with his fans. He can show off egg-cellent new abilities, with giant eggs called mega eggdozer and metal eggdozer now part of his dino destruction tools. Yoshi's goal is to reunite Baby Mario with Baby Luigi – his flutter wings are also a crucial new item!

SECRET IDENTITY

It's not really known what creature Yoshi is. Some players think he's a pre-historic dinosaur, there are rumours he may be a giant lizard and some signs in *Super Mario Galaxy 2* describe Yoshi as a dragon. Keep playing his games and maybe one day you'll discover the truth!

19

#5 DAISY

The ruler of Sarasland, Daisy is another royal subject with major abilities and influence in the Mushroom Kingdom. Take a trip through her best moments!

PRECIOUS PRINCESS

Daisy isn't always known as Princess Daisy in her on-screen roles, but she is proper Nintendo royalty. Not much is known about her home nation, Sarasland, except for that it neighbours Mushroom Kingdom and has four regions. Daisy entered the Super Mario world in 1989's *Super Mario Land* game.

POPULAR PLAYER

Daisy has popped up in more than 70 Nintendo videogames since 1989!

PEACH PERFECT

Often compared to Princess Peach, it's fair to say Daisy is more of a tomboy than her pink pal and takes part in sporty contests with a ruthless winning streak. She will often bust out her showboating moves after a victory, especially if she outsmarts the evil Waluigi!

FLOWER POWER

Most of her special moves involve flowers and plants. In *Mario Tennis Aces*, watch out for Daisy's bloom blast and her trail of petals during play. She is a tough opponent in *Super Smash Bros. Ultimate*, using a summoning of daisies to get the better of other fighters. This princess is no soft touch!

ENEMY TARGET

Why does Waluigi have a history with Princess Daisy? The pair are big rivals on the tennis court and the purple pest can't stand losing to her! They face-off with each other again in *Mario Kart 8* and *Mario Strikers Charged*, with bad feelings between the pair. Perhaps Waluigi secretly loves her?!

3 FUN FACTS

1 A Baby Daisy character is in Mario Super Sluggers!

2 Daisy loves flowers... she is named after one!

3 Daisy is rumoured to be Luigi's love interest!

ULTIMATE APPEARANCE

Daisy makes a great entrance in *Super Smash Bros. Ultimate*. It's the first time she becomes a playable character. In this game she teams up with Peach as an echo fighter, which is a cool new fighting function where Daisy copies all of Peach's major moves. It's a total royal rumble!

COURSE YOU CAN

Race through the Daisy Hills and Daisy Cruiser courses in *Mario Kart 7*. Daisy Cruiser is part of the Flower Cup and Leaf Cup and is an awesome circuit set on a cruise ship with hazards at every turn. The karting glider system was first used in this game, taking Daisy to new racing heights!

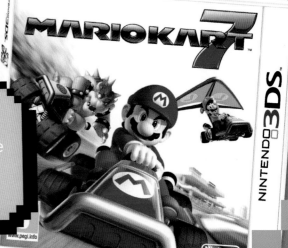

#6 ROSALINA

A visitor from another galaxy? Rosalina may seem on a different level to her friends, but really she's a good girl to have in the Mario group!

BIG STAR

Rosalina made her debut in *Super Mario Galaxy* in 2007. Another Nintendo princess, she is literally a videogame star because she's the adopted mum of the star-shaped Luma characters! This lady is a protective presence in the Galaxy and a great guide for Mario and the rest.

FORCEFUL LADY

Rosalina's secret gift is her forcefield. She can protect the Comet Observatory in *Super Mario Galaxy* with her strong shield, which also has transportation powers. Her wand is packed with magical abilities too, making Rosalina a cosmic force capable of amazing strikes during attacks.

DAZZLING LOOK

If you confuse her with Daisy and Peach, perhaps the wave of stars that can follow her around will help to identify Rosalina! Usually she has a power style in sports games, with a big smash hit in tennis and golf. The princess is suited to all sorts of battles, mixing strength with intelligence and swift reactions.

CAPPY #7

A Super Mario character who is 'heading' for the top! Check out the coolest info and secrets about one of Mario's newest friends.

CAPPY'S CRUSADE

Cappy's first adventure with Mario came in *Super Mario Odyssey* on Switch. He comes from the Cap Kingdom and takes the look of Mario's famous red hat. This dude loves zooming through the air and has amazing powers to help defeat Bowser's latest attempt to snatch Princess Peach!

HAT TRICKS

Mario can use Cappy for loads of awesome moves in the *Odyssey* game. A well-placed throw will wipe out enemies, a special spin throw catches the baddies by surprise and there's also Cappy's levitation powers, allowing Mario to rise up and reach new levels. The hat tricks are endless!

CAP-TASTIC

As well as sitting on Mario's head and transforming his skills in *Odyssey*, other cap-tastic machines and creatures appear. Sherm is a tough tank with a red cap, which can be captured and used for good things. Watch out for the T-Rex too – a terrifying dino with a silly-looking red hat!

#8 PAULINE

The special character in a red outfit, Pauline is back with a bang in the Mario universe! This lady means business, so don't get in her way!

MAYOR PAULINE

Pauline was Mario's original love interest – she was in the *Donkey Kong* arcade games of the early 1980s! She disappeared for a long time, but made a great comeback for Nintendo in the *Mario vs Donkey Kong* games from 2007 onwards. Pauline has a big role in *Super Mario Odyssey* as the mayor of New Donk City!

BUSY LADY

Pauline is always a target for Donkey Kong and that's why Mario seeks to save and protect her. She is a clever lady with a business brain. Pauline loves singing in her band and has made guest appearances in *Mario Kart*, *Mario Tennis Aces* and *Mario Strikers Battle League*. After her long time away from videogames, she's now here to stay as another powerful Mario pal!

ARE YOU RED-Y?

Pauline dresses in lots of exciting outfits and clothes... but always in red!

LUMAS

#9

Light up your screen with the lovely Lumas!

GALAXY ENTRANCE

Number nine in the list of Mario's fantastic friends are the Lumas. These adorable tear-shaped stars glittered on the *Super Mario Galaxy* adventures and their main job is transforming into planets and galaxies. Impressive! Mainly yellow, Lumas can also be found in blue, pink, green and red.

LUMA LEADER

Wanna meet the Lumas' boss? As well as being ruled by Rosalina, a puffed-up character called Lubba reckons he's the leader of the Luma Crew. All these creatures come from the head-shaped Starship Mario planet – there's plenty of intergalactic action going on!

STAR TIP!
Don't confuse Lumas with the more pointy Power Stars or Shine Sprites!

#10 BIRDO

Mario may not see much of Birdo, but when she pops up it puts a smile on his face!

RARE SIGHT

The pink dino is a treat to find when she appears in Mario games! Birdo has over 30 years' experience in videogames but can still be a rare find. You may see her with Yoshi, another creature like her, and she lurks in the background in *Mario Kart, Super Smash Bros.* and tennis and golf scenes. As a playable character she's quite a force!

DINO DELIGHT

New gamers often take a step back from Birdo. Unsure if she's a genuine friend, her appearance can be a worry at first. There's no need to panic really, because this pretty creature always acts in good faith for the Super Mario cause.

25

MARIO QUIZ

Take the test to see how much you really know about the action hero!

?

1
What was Mario originally known as?

A. Leapman

B. Jumpman

C. Bounceman

2
Where does Mario live?

A. Mushroom City

B. Mushroom Land

C. Mushroom Kingdom

3
In which year did Mario first appear?

A. 1971

B. 1981

C. 1991

4
Which of these is NOT a real Mario game?

A. Super Mario Smash

B. Super Mario 64

C. Super Mario Odyssey

5 In *Luigi's Mansion*, what is Mario trapped inside?

A. A painting ☐

B. A bathroom ☐

C. A prison ☐

6 On which date is Mario celebrated each year?

A. April 1 ☐

B. March 1 ☐

C. March 10 ☐

8 Which of these is a Mario Kart 8 spin-off game?

A. *Mario Kart 8 Speed* ☐

B. *Mario Kart 8 Deluxe* ☐

C. *Mario Kart 8 Full Throttle* ☐

7 What was the first Olympic Games that Mario and Sonic teamed up for?

A. 2008 ☐

B. 2012 ☐

C. 2016 ☐

9 In Mario games, what does the abbreviation 'bros.' actually mean?

A. Brothers ☐

B. Brownstone ☐

C. Brontosaurus ☐

10 Who is the tallest out of these three stars?

A. Toad ☐

B. Mario ☐

C. Yoshi ☐

ANSWERS ON PAGE 78

NINTENDO NUMBERS

Speed through these cool and fun-filled numbers and facts all about Nintendo...

767

Nintendo star Sonic the Hedgehog is rumoured to dash at a staggering **767 miles per hour**. That's the same as the speed of sound!

40,000,000,000

Nintendo is a giant Japanese company worth more than **£40,000,000,000**. If you don't know what all the zeroes mean, it's £40 billion!

35

In 2020, Nintendo released **Super Mario Bros. 35** as part of the game's 35th anniversary. It had 35-player battles with 35 seconds to succeed!

52,000,000

Mario Kart 8 Deluxe is the biggest-selling videogame of all time on Nintendo Switch. It has sold over **52 million copies!**

10

Nintendo celebrates a special Mario Day every year on March 10. They call it 'MAR10' Day – what an awesome event!

2,807

That's the **number of Lego pieces** making up the Mighty Bowser brick-built toy. Lego and Mario are a great combination!

1992

In 1992, catchy tunes called **Supermarioland** and *Tetris*, based on the huge Game Boy game, entered the UK song charts. Videogame fans loved the music!

5,000

So far, more than **5,000 different videogames** have been made for all the awesome Nintendo consoles since the 1980s!

1,100,000 +

New videogames may be a bit expensive, but even old ones can cost a fortune. An original version of *Super Mario 64*, from 1996, sold for **£1.1 million** at auction in 2022!

CONSOLE COUNTDOWN

How well do you know your Nintendo history? Here's a rapid rundown of all the greatest consoles.

COLOR TV-GAME

YEAR: 1977
TOP GAMES: Various

In the 1970s, Nintendo worked mega hard to gain control of the home console industry. It's first real machine for this was the Color TV-Game. Each version could play just one simple game, such as a basic tennis match or racing event. Around three million sold in Japan!

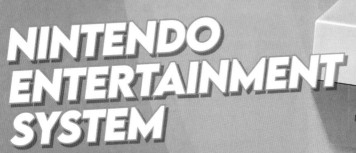

NINTENDO ENTERTAINMENT SYSTEM

YEAR: 1985
TOP GAMES: Super Mario Bros., Metroid, The Legend of Zelda

This home console smashed it in the 1980s, eventually reaching 70 million homes around the world! With clever tech and a cool look for the time, the Nintendo Entertainment System was the first that could load different games. It was like having an arcade machine in your bedroom!

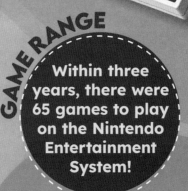

GAME RANGE

Within three years, there were 65 games to play on the Nintendo Entertainment System!

GAME BOY

YEAR: 1989
TOP GAMES: Tetris, Super Mario Land

Game Boy was another legendary computer that made Nintendo the coolest videogame company. The first handheld device, this meant games could finally be played on the move and fans never had to be without the buzz of Mario and other Nintendo heroes!

SUPER NINTENDO ENTERTAINMENT SYSTEM

YEAR: 1992
TOP GAMES: The Legend of Zelda: A Link to the Past, Super Mario World

Known as the SNES, this home console sparked another computing craze and was a massive hit with gamers around the globe! Faster and sleeker than the original NES, it was so popular that Nintendo created the SNES Classic edition in 2017!

NINTENDO 64

YEAR: 1996
TOP GAMES: Super Mario 64, Mario Kart 64, GoldenEye 007

Competing with the Sony PlayStation console, Nintendo 64 had an awesome controller, plus graphics and sound that took gaming to new heights. *Mario Kart 64* was a high-speed blast and the Pokémon games came to a home console for the first time.

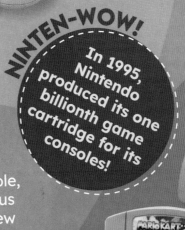

NINTEN-WOW!

In 1995, Nintendo produced its one billionth game cartridge for its consoles!

GAME BOY COLOR

YEAR: 1998
TOP GAMES: Tetris DX, Wario Land II

If the original grey Game Boy wasn't flashy enough for you, the bright purple Game Boy Color would be! The handheld console was still really popular with great games to choose, plus the new Game Boy Camera device attached to the back of it.

NINTENDO GAMECUBE

YEAR: 2001
TOP GAMES: Luigi's Mansion, Super Smash Bros. Melee

GameCube was exactly that – a cool console that looked like a cube! Nintendo had lots of great titles available for the machine, including *Luigi's Mansion* and *Sonic Adventure 2*. GameCube sold over 21 million around the world between 2001 to 2007.

DOUBLE DELIGHT

The Mario Kart: Double Dash!! GameCube game saw two racers on a kart for the first time!

GAME BOY ADVANCE

YEAR: 2001
TOP GAMES: Super Mario Advance, F-Zero: Maximum Velocity

The Game Boy had a major reboot with the all-new Advance model in 2001. Very different to the original, GBA was another big success for Nintendo, selling 81.5 million in total and giving gamers even more power in their hands!

NINTENDO DS

YEAR: 2004
TOP GAMES: Animal Crossing: Wild World, Metroid Prime HUNTERS

The DS, and its follow-ups the 3DS and DSi, became a gamechanger for Nintendo! The dual-screen tech and WiFi link-up was huge at the time and there were hundreds of games to pick from. From grandkids to great grannies, everyone could play on the brilliant DS!

NINTENDO Wii

YEAR: 2006
TOP GAMES: Wii Sports, The Legend of Zelda: Twilight Princess

Wii Sports games meant players entered a virtual world, smashing a tennis ball or playing ten-pin bowling while standing in front of the screen! The Wii was an amazing and fun console, selling over 100 million and keeping Nintendo top of the gaming entertainment industry for several years.

NINTENDO Wii U

YEAR: 2012
TOP GAMES: New Super Mario Bros. U, Nintendo Land

The Wii U GamePad controller used a clever integrated second screen, making this handheld version of the Wii a must-have for gaming fans! It set the way for the launch of the mighty Switch in a few years' time. It only sold around 13 million, though, which actually makes the Wii U quite a rare console.

NINTENDO SWITCH

YEAR: 2017
TOP GAMES: Mario Kart 8 Deluxe, Super Smash Bros. Ultimate

The Switch really did switch up the gaming world from 2017 onwards! Called a 'hybrid' console, because it was a portable tablet that could be docked and connected to a screen, the special joy-con controllers gives players so much option for exploring new games. A massive 120 million Switch consoles are already being loaded up and enjoyed around the planet!

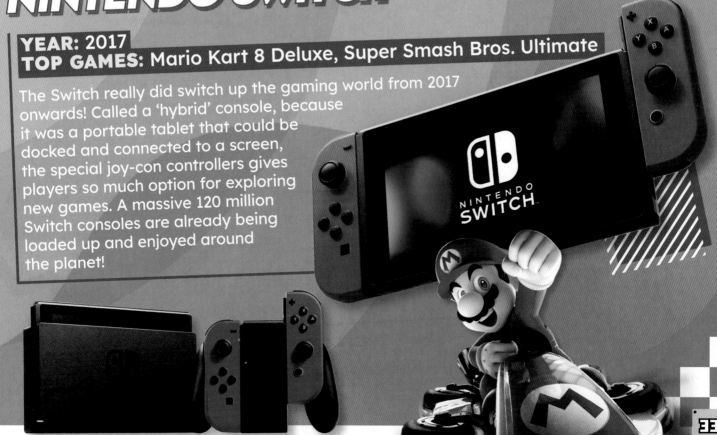

BOWSER

#1

Time to be brave and take on Mario's ten biggest Nintendo enemies! There's only one place to begin and that's Bowser – the ultimate baddie!

KOOPA KING

Bowser is a large turtle-like Koopa creature who causes misery throughout Mushroom Kingdom. As the King of the Koopas, he rules with terror and when Bowser's missions don't go to plan, he's not happy. He regularly targets Princess Peach, leaving Mario to strike back and beat Bowser and his troublesome gang!

INSIDE STORY

A regular baddie in the Super Mario world since the 1980s, Bowser finally got named in a game when *Mario & Luigi: Bowser's Inside Story* came out in 2009. Bowser eats a mushroom and begins sucking in all the people around him, including Mario and Luigi. The brothers have to escape from inside Bowser's body. Urgh!

NINTENDO DS.

MARIO & LUIGI BOWSER'S INSIDE STORY

3

BOG BATTLE

Have you played *Super Mario 3D World + Bowser's Fury*? It's a frantic Switch game where you and a friend fight back against a giant-sized, ultra-scary version of Bowser! The evildoer is bigger and badder than ever before – use all your skills to stop him!

1 He has a ridiculous plan to marry Princess Peach!

2 There's a cat version of him called Meowser!

3 Bowser's size changes a lot in different games!

COMMANDING CREATURE

Bowser has plenty of power and muscle to damage Mario, but the army of supporters he commands makes him even more formidable! Koopas, Bullet Bills and Shy Guys are all under his spell, so think twice and plan ahead before taking on this mighty creature.

QUICK THINKING

Bowser is big and often slow moving, but don't think he lacks brains and quick thinking. This destructive dude is determined to win and will adapt to his surroundings, using machines and weapons to get the upper hand. Remember that he breathes fire as well!

SAVE HIM!?

Always be prepared for new twists and adventures when dealing with Bowser! The *Mario & Luigi: Superstar Saga + Bowser's Minions* game has a mini section where you lead the Captain Goomba character in actually saving Bowser. It feels so strange being nice towards the Koopa King!

#2 DONKEY KONG

Swing and bash your way to victory, just like the destructive Donkey Kong! Find out about the most amazing ape in the Nintendo world...

+ >>>

HISTORY LESSON

The great ape has been on the scene since the very first days with Mario in the 1980s. Donkey Kong was meant to be the first Nintendo character to dominate arcades and consoles, but Mario soon took the spotlight. Here's the big question: is Donkey Kong a baddie or a goodie?

GOOD vs BAD

Donkey Kong started out doing evil tasks and being mean to Mario. Over the years, he has sometimes become a helpful hero to the brothers, using his power and bravery for good causes. DK is never far from trouble though, like when he snatches Pauline in *Mario vs Donkey Kong: Tipping Stars*!

MARIO VS DONKEY KONG™ Tipping Stars

KONG KING

Donkey Kong, or 'DK' to those who know him best, is the leader of the Kong species that come from Donkey Kong Island. Take a tour through the Switch game *Donkey Kong Country: Tropical Freeze* to explore this interesting island. Watch out for the Snowmads putting you in deep freeze danger!

1 Over 20 million DK games have been sold!

2 His son is called Donkey Kong Jr!

3 Check out the DK initials on his red tie!

BEST FRIEND

Donkey Kong can't always win by himself. Luckily, he calls on Diddy Kong to enter levels, puzzles and battles alongside him! This mini ape is DK's top friend. Even though he doesn't have Donkey Kong's strength, Diddy makes up for that with speed, agility and jumping power. He's a mega pri-mate!

CROC CLASH

Donkey Kong doesn't just tangle with Mario. His ultimate opponent is a crazy croc called King K. Rool! In *DK: King of Swing*, the croc swipes medals from Donkey Kong and in the Donkey Kong Jungle Climber game, King K. Rool goes bananas and scraps many times with the ape!

BANANA ACTION

As you might expect, many of Donkey Kong's adventures and contests are based around bananas. The guy loves 'em! Often his stash of bananas goes missing and DK's rage rises, but other times mysterious banana-based characters appear and he has to outsmart them!

37

#3 WARIO

Mario faces many rivals in the Nintendo world, but not many are as evil as Wario. Discover why this crazy character is a nasty piece of work!

GET TOGETHER

The Wario Ware range of games are totally wacky – just like the man himself! In *Wario Ware: Get It Together,* for Switch, you control Wario and his pals in loads of bonkers minigames. Meet up with 18-Volt, Mona, Dr. Crygor, Mike and others in this manic mash-up of on-screen activities!

MANIC MOVES

Wario unleashes a fierce fart attack move in *Super Smash Bros. Brawl.* It's totally gross! Technically this attack is called the Wario Waft, but it's proof that spending too much time with such a stinkin' bad guy is not good for your health.

KART CHAOS

Wario has been in every Mario Kart game apart from the 1980s original. His transport usually has decent top speed and slower acceleration. In *Mario Kart Wii* game, things are totally flipped, because his Wario bike rips up awesome acceleration but a rubbish top speed. Wario always keeps you guessing!

GOOD LOOKING

Have you noticed how Wario thinks a lot of himself in Nintendo games? As well as cooking up trouble, he takes time to check his look because he reckons he's handsome and attractive. Errr... what kind of mirror is he looking at?!

3 FUN FACTS

1 Rumour has it that Wario is a plumber, like Mario!

2 He's obsessed by money – even other people's!

3 Wario loves garlic, so his breath is minging!

FASHION FORCE

The *Wario: Master of Disguise* game proves that he loves to look after himself and dress in fancy gear! Players put him in different costumes that grant great powers, such as Cosmic Wario's laser blasts and Thief Wario's tackles. He also teams up with a new magical wand that gives him top tricks in how to disguise!

WORSHIP WARIO?

If, for some reason, you're a fan of the weird Wario character, then treat yourself to a trip to some of his named locations and even get inside some of his special outfits. There's the Mount Wario track in *Mario Kart 8 Deluxe*, as well as the Wario cowboy and Wario hiker gear.

WALUIGI

#4

Whenever Wario is on the scene, you can be sure Waluigi is not far behind. Here's a rundown of this sneaky Nintendo star!

BLAST OFF!

His 'whirluigi' tennis shot has a powerful cyclone effect on the court!

MARIO MENACE

You could describe Waluigi as a bit of a millennium bug – he arrived in the year 2000 and has been a pain ever since! Waluigi is Wario's sidekick and together they torment and annoy Mario, Luigi and the rest of the good-natured Nintendo group. This lanky, purple dude should be avoided at all costs!

TENNIS ACE

Waluigi's first appearance was in the *Mario Tennis* game as a doubles partner for his pal, Wario. He has strong technique and reach but not great speed covering the court. In *Mario Tennis Aces* on Switch, the pair serve up lots of problems in the action-packed Adventure mode!

FUN FACTS

1 Waluigi has a crush on Daisy!

2 His long legs and arms are great for sport!

3 Waluigi has an upside down 'L' on his cap!

FAMILY FORCE

Most people think that, like Mario and Luigi, Waluigi and Wario are brothers. But, they're actually just partners in crime and not related. Play *Mario Kart Double: Double Dash*!! and they pair up together to race. Throwing an explosive Bob-omb is their special move!

SPORTY STAR

Watch out for Waluigi in any sports showdown – he's a fierce player and hates losing! Whether he teams up with Wario, goes head-to-head with Luigi or just sets his sights on victory he will do anything to win. From ice hockey and skating to baseball and golf, he's a big threat!

SERIOUS BUSINESS

Waluigi wants to be taken seriously, with gamers treating him as the evil genius he dreams of being. But with Waluigi's silly moustache, his awkward arms and legs and an attitude that stinks, it's tough to give him the respect he demands. Sorry!

#5 KOOPA TROOPA

Number five on Mario's enemy list are the Koopa Troopas – a turtle-y difficult opponent to outsmart in the Mushroom Kingdom!

SUPER TROOPAS

Look out for the Koopa Troopas stomping through the Mushroom Kingdom! They are an army of troublesome turtle-tastic creatures, guided by Bowser as part of the Koopa Troop. They may look cute and cuddly, but get close and these soldiers will strike hard!

SHELLING OUT

Koopa Troopas are a classic part of Mario Kart. Just like the shell on their back, they love to unleash a triple shell special move and create a protective barrier around their vehicle. This gives them a vital advantage in racing to the finish line!

SKY HIGH

Flying Koopa Troopas with wings are the special Koopa Paratroopas. Often seen with red and green shells, these flighty foes turn back into regular Troopas if they are stomped on in the air. They pop up in *Super Mario Bros.*, *Mario Kart*, *Super Smash Bros.* and loads more games!

KOOPLINGS

Don't mix up the Koopa Troopas with the Koopalings. Also known as the Koopa Kids, the Koopalings are Bowser's minions and they get together to carry out his nasty plans. There are seven Koopalings, called Larry, Ludwig, Morton, Wendy, Iggy, Roy and Lemmy. Keep an eye on these crazy kids in the Super Mario universe!

3 FUN FACTS

1 Koopa Troopas were called Shellcreepers at first!

2 Often known as just Koopas or Troopas!

3 They hide in their shell when scared!

SCARY SIGHT!

The skeleton remains of Koopa Troopas are the Dry Bones, found in places like deserts and castles!

LETHAL LOOK-A-LIKES

The Koopalings look like regular Koopa Troopas and they have many shared powers. They first appear as playable characters in *Mario Kart 8*, causing high-speed problems with every twist and turn they make on the track!

#6 BOWSER JR

Nintendo's mini Bowser is just like his dad, with menacing strength and a mission to take control of Mushroom Kingdom!

MINI ME

Bowser's one and only son, Bowser Jr. showed up in the *Super Mario Sunshine* game. Although small, he's still strong and is even rumoured to be smarter than his dad! The first time he was named in a game title was for *Mario & Luigi: Bowser's Inside Story + Bowser Jr.'s Journey* in 2019.

JR.'S JOURNEY

In *Bowser Jr.'s Journey*, he guides his squad of soldiers as they battle the fearsome Fawful character. Helped by the Koopalings and the magical Kamek, he searches for mysterious medicine and must take advantage of in-game boosts like beans, protective shield and a lightning strike!

BAD DAD

Jr. and Bowser make a powerful pair when they team up on console games, whether that's racing in Mario Kart or smashing shots in the Tennis games. His short arms mean he struggles to reach objects, but he's quick and prepared to do anything to win!

GOOMBA

Are these fungus also fun guys around Mario? No way – the Goombas try to cause mischief everywhere they march!

SCARY STUFF?

Another member of the Koopa Troop, Goombas reckon they are scary and troublesome, when actually just a little jump over them usually does the trick! They look fearsome even if a Goomba doesn't deal out much destruction in the Mushroom Kingdom!

GOOMBA SPECIES

There are several sub species of Goombas in the Nintendo universe. Cat Goomba, Gold Goomba, Bone Goomba and winged Paragoombas all appear at times to be annoying for Mario and his friends. As a part of pretty much every Mario game there's no escape from them!

TOWER MOVE

In *Super Mario Odyssey*, look out for Goombas linking up in a smart move. Known as a Goomba tower, they can jump on top of each other and create a tall structure that looks very worrying for other players around them. Goombas are much better as a team!

FRIENDLY FIRST

Goombas were once friendly Mushroom Kingdom characters before joining the Koopa Troop!

#8 BOO

Prepare for a ghostly surprise as the Boos enter the countdown of evil Nintendo enemies!

GHOSTLY STORY

Nintendo officially describes them as "mischievous" – Mario and Luigi can't stand the scary sight of them! To be fair, the Boo ghosts look much worse than they really are, because this species is also very shy and will cover their faces if someone stares at them.

TERRIFYING TALK

The Boos speak in a language called Booish!

KING BOO

This is the leader of the Boos! The most powerful ghost has no respect for Luigi and believes all others should bow down before his royal spirit. As well as having regular Boo abilities, the King can also open paranormal portals, create traps and fire epic lasers!

LUIGI RIVAL

Beware – if you play *Luigi's Mansion* then the Boos are everywhere! Luigi must destroy them with the Poltergust as he explores the horror house. They move around in the dark and will try to escape whenever Luigi is on the prowl. Aim the vacuum at their long tongue and reel 'em in!

BOB-OMB #9

The most explosive of Mario's enemies! Take cover when these destructive foes are on the scene.

SPECIAL ATTENTION

Don't take your eyes off the Bob-ombs! They are packed with power and deserve to be kept at a distance. Bob-ombs have been around since the 1980s and show up all the time in hundreds of games, from platform adventures to racing events and on-screen battles.

KART-ASTROPHE

Bob-ombs have been known to chase Mario and Luigi, but they usually just cause an explosion when they get annoyed by their opponents. In Mario Kart, Bob-ombs can be thrown and will follow an enemy kart and then blow up on contact. They make a very helpful item!

#10 SHY GUY

Don't be shy, because these little creatures won't do Mario and Luigi any harm... or will they?!

MASKED MENACE

Why do Shy Guys wear huge masks? Because they're extremely shy and need to cover their face! Not as common as other Mario enemies, they can be a pesky presence and will show up on a kart track, tennis court or a golf course to disrupt the day. Shy Guys are a pain when they team up together!

BOSS HELP

Shy Guys have worked with a few enemy bosses, from Bowser to the magical Kamek, but their lack of bravery is always their downfall. They have few special abilities and often just rely on running at Mario and Luigi to cause disruption. If you think they are cute and cuddly, then think again!

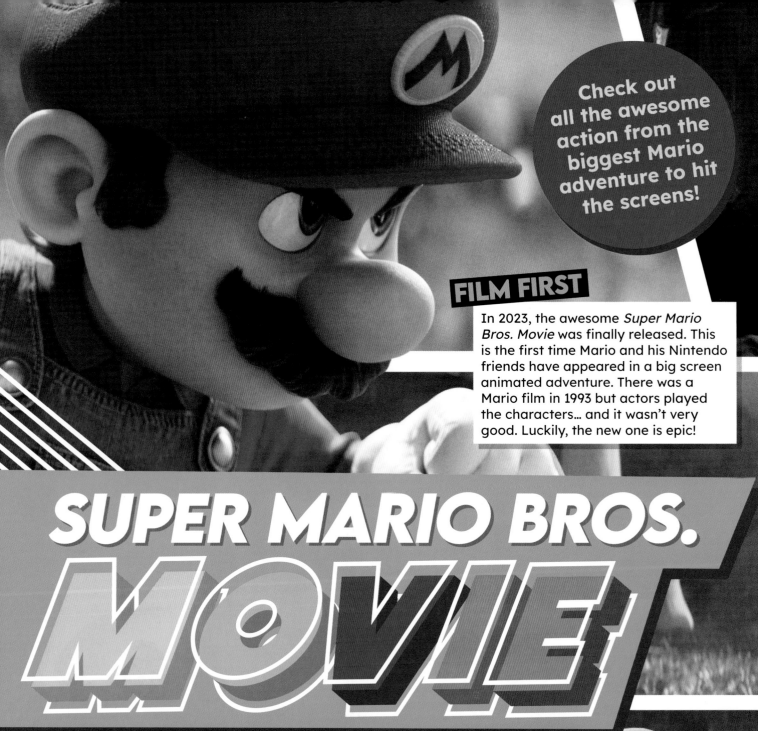

Check out all the awesome action from the biggest Mario adventure to hit the screens!

FILM FIRST

In 2023, the awesome *Super Mario Bros. Movie* was finally released. This is the first time Mario and his Nintendo friends have appeared in a big screen animated adventure. There was a Mario film in 1993 but actors played the characters… and it wasn't very good. Luckily, the new one is epic!

SUPER MARIO BROS. MOVIE

HOLLYWOOD HEROES

Superhero actor Chris Pratt, who stars in Marvel's *Guardians of the Galaxy* and *Jurassic World*, is the fun voice of Mario. Jack Black voices Bowser, Seth Rogen plays Donkey Kong and Charlie Day brings Luigi to life!

GAME ON

Watching the *Super Mario Bros. Movie* is a bit like seeing your favourite Mario games played out on the screen! With karts, motorbikes, obstacles, puzzles and Luigi having to face down his fears, you'll love every second of the movie mayhem!

PEACH POWER

Princess Peach, ruler of the Kingdom, battles alongside Mario every step of the way. Luigi, Toad and Donkey Kong are also never far away from the heated fight. You'll soon see that not every plan runs smoothly, though!

NINTENDO WORLD

Set in the magical Mushroom Kingdom made famous in Mario games, the evil monster Bowser is once again the biggest threat to the safety of the universe. Mario and his pals have a major mission to stop him!

TROUBLED TIMES

Lots of fearsome Nintendo foes feature in the film. Look out for Koopas creating carnage, Kamek causing chaos and Spikes doing their best to spoil Mario's mission. The bad guys and girls are super tough to stop!

49

NINTENDO QUIZ

Take ten fun questions all about
the world of Nintendo!
Fill in your answer in the space.

01 Who is the King of
the Koopas?

+

Nintendo

02 The Nintendo company first
started in which country?

03 Can you name this
scary thing?

04 Which crafty character
thinks he's very handsome?

05 Re-arrange these letters to spell a famous Nintendo game:
T E R S I T

06 Together Larry, Ludwig, Morton, Wendy, Iggy, Roy and Lemmy are known as the what?

07 These annoying brown creatures are the...

08 What do the initials 'SNES' mean?

09 In which year did the Nintendo Switch come out?

10 What type of 'snappy' animal is King K. Rool?

ANSWERS ON PAGE 78

Check out some of the biggest and best Mario games of all time!

MARIO KART 8 DELUXE

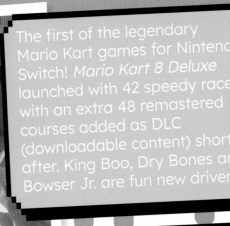

The first of the legendary Mario Kart games for Nintendo Switch! *Mario Kart 8 Deluxe* launched with 42 speedy racers, with an extra 48 remastered courses added as DLC (downloadable content) shortly after. King Boo, Dry Bones and Bowser Jr. are fun new drivers.

Join the renegade round-up battle mode for a dangerous duel with the best Mario Kart racers! One team tries to capture the other and place them in prison. Remember to think fast and bust your pals out of jail by pressing the button under the jail cell!

Need a sneaky way to beat the rest? In *Mario Kart 8 Deluxe*, racers can hold two items instead of just one. Unleash a wicked green shell and slide a banana skin to put the brakes on the chasing pack!

TOP TIP!

Use the Boo item to turn invisible!

If you're new to the mega Mario Kart world or just need a little help to grab a top-three spot, simply use the new smart steering control option. This function keeps you firmly on the fast track as you blitz by your rivals!

MARIO + RABBIDS SPARK OF HOPE

The fantastic follow-up to the 2017 hit *Mario + Rabbids Kingdom Battle, Sparks of Hope* takes the moustached hero on one of his fiercest journeys! Players must collect and protect the Sparks – powerful creatures formed by the mixing of Lumas and Rabbids. It's epic!

Build a team of top Nintendo stars to battle in the galaxy! Select from Mario, Rabbid Mario, Peach, Rabbid Peach, Rabbid Rosalina, Luigi, Rabbid Luigi, Bowser and Edge. Edge is a new hero who is cool, confident and ready to do anything to keep the Sparks safe!

Be prepared to face Cursa – the evil spirit chasing the Sparks and spreading a dangerous substance called Darkmess. The Sparks each have special skills and players must use their power and bonus ability to outwit Cursa.

Starburst, Reflector, Pyrostar, Twinkle, Aquanox and Toxiquake are just some of the Sparks. Whether you get a speed or a strength increase, use it at the right moment and remember there's a cooldown time afterwards. Dash and team jump your enemies to take a glorious victory in the galaxy!

SUPER MARIO ODYSSEY

This time, the Mushroom Kingdom is left behind as Mario enters the amazing Odyssey airship to explore new lands. His mission is to catch up with Bowser, because once again he's snatched Peach and plans to marry her. Luckily, Mario's new friend Cappy has great powers!

The Cappy character has cool jumps and throws to help Mario beat the baddies. The Odyssey needs power moon items as its primary energy source. Look for these throughout the land, or pay for them at the Crazy Cap shop.

Collect unique coins in each of the kingdoms, including Metro, Sand, Luncheon, Wooded and Cascade. These can only be spent in each specific location, though. Look for the coins high and low and if there's an open door, be brave enough to pass through it!

TOP TIP!

Outfit changes look good, but they don't grant Mario any new powers!

At first, use the assist mode to quickly get to grips with *Super Mario Odyssey*. You'll see helpful arrows showing where to go, damage won't be as harmful and you can spawn again from the same spot. Once you're a pro player, exit assist mode and take on the full challenge!

MARIO STRIKERS BATTLE LEAGUE

In *Mario Strikers Battle League*, your aim is to be victorious on the pitch and build the universe's top club. So, what's the sport in this popular Switch game? It's called strike – a frantic five-versus-five team event that's a bit like football, but with less rules and a lot more fighting. Ouch!

Pick your team of star Mushroom Kingdom players. Pay attention to their prime skills as well. Peach has high speed and top technique, Toad is an expert passer and Boom Boom operates as a quality keeper. You need a team packed with all-round powers!

TOP TIP!

Look out for the electric fence around the field. It's a shocking feature!

When you play games you collect coins. Coins are vital in *Battle League*, because you can then trade gear for your head, arms, body and legs. New suits to match your player's battle style is a great way to get a winning team!

Each player has a unique move called a hyper strike. For example, Mario's hyper strike is the fire cyclone and Luigi rocks the spin tornado. It's well worth getting a successful hyper strike, because it's a game changer worth TWO goals instead of just one!

MARIO PARTY SUPERSTARS

Fans of classic boardgames and minigames can't get enough of *Mario Party Superstars*! It has so many puzzles, problems, challenges and activities to master, you'll be playing it for years. It's based on five popular boardgames from the legendary Nintendo 64 era.

Visit Peach's Birthday Cake, Space Land, Yoshi's Tropical Island, Horror Land and Woody Woods. Birthday Cake is a sweet place, with strawberry plants growing into Piranha plants, but there's a different vibe in Space Land. Look for runaway spacecraft and Bowser's coin beam!

There are 100 fun minigames, in categories such as four-player free-for-alls, one-versus-three or duel. Pick a challenge from the sports & puzzles section and you'll soon be breaking blocks in Mario's Party Puzzle. Take advantage of the falling Thwomps that squash blocks for you!

↓96 yd.

Unsurprisingly, getting stars is an important part of *Mario Party Superstars*! In some games, getting the most stars makes you the winner. Set the pre-game stats to decide how many stars each player begins with and use the minigame practise to perfect your skills.

TOP TIP!
In the trio challenge, a team needs five wins in a row to clear a stage. Tricky!

SUPER MARIO 3D WORLD + BOWSER'S FURY

The Sprixie Kingdom is the setting in this 2021 release from the *Super Mario 3D World* series! Joined by Peach, Toad and Luigi, Mario faces Bowser in a colourful and chaotic clash. You'll be zooming through river rapids and skating across icy scenes as the hero of the hour!

Always stay clued-up on the abilities and risks of each player. Peach's mid-air float gives her a safe landing, but she's slower than the rest. Toad brings speed and while Luigi has a height advantage, he takes a little while to get his speed and direction under control.

Use power-ups to help you take control. The double cherry makes a clone copy of your character, launch hot strikes with fire flower and the mega mushroom has truly gigantic power – the opposition will taste a crushing defeat from this!

TOP TIP!

Unlock the Rosalina character by completing the main 3D World game!

Bowser's Fury is a thrilling extra adventure with this Switch title. You partner with Bowser Jr. to stop his dark and destructive oversized dad! Collect five cat shines to trigger the giga bell and steer Bowser Jr.'s Koopa clown car to save the day!

MARIO KART LIVE: HOME CIRCUIT

One of the smartest, coolest and cleverest Mario games ever! Mario and Luigi kart figures are placed on the floor of your living room or bedroom and by using the Switch controls, they move through a virtual circuit that you create. The action is seen on your Switch or TV!

Use the four special gates to make your racing track, which could be a traditional oval circuit or a twisty figure of eight. Courses come to life with settings such as jungle, snowscape and sandstorm. Steer clear of the dreaded enemies, including Piranha plants and Thwomps!

Join in with eight grand prix cup events and take on the Koopalings and other characters. The track you've built is displayed by virtual lines on your screen, so you always know what turns to make. Just don't bash into any furniture in your room!

Always aim for an item box to give you a chance of getting an item. Red shells, bananas, spiny shells, lightning, bullet bills... these all impact your drive and the other racers around you in this crazy virtual dash!

TOP TIP!

Select racing modes from 50cc up to a fast-paced 200cc!

NEW SUPER MARIO BROS. U DELUXE

With over 160 courses, *New Super Mario Bros. U Deluxe* has a classic platform feel, but amazing graphics and interactivity. Track down coins, defeat a bunch of enemies and search for the goal pole in a 2D-style game that still leaps out of your Switch screen!

Mario has Toad and Luigi for company as usual, but there are two new heroes to meet. Toadette has lots of skills and if she powers-up with a super crown, she'll change into Peachette! Check out Nabbit as well, a character who will not suffer enemy damage.

Fancy some cool power-ups in *New Super Mario Bros. U Deluxe*? Freeze enemies with ice balls, transform to a tiny being thanks to the mini mushroom and become a flying squirrel by using the eye-catching nut item. These abilities are a big boost!

TOP TIP!

Balloon Baby Yoshi, Bubble Baby Yoshi and Glowing Baby Yoshi all make fun appearances!

A spin-off game, called *New Super Luigi U*, also comes as part of this epic adventure. It's the first time he has a starring role in a platform-type game. With even tougher tasks and just 100 seconds to do it, the race is on to get the goal pole before time runs out!

MARIO GOLF: SUPER RUSH

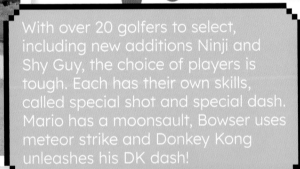

Get your golf clubs ready and hit the fairways in the exciting *Mario Golf: Super Rush* game! From speed golf mode to golf adventure and even full-on battle golf, there's a setting to tee off your sporting challenge as Mario and his mates are in full swing!

With over 20 golfers to select, including new additions Ninji and Shy Guy, the choice of players is tough. Each has their own skills, called special shot and special dash. Mario has a moonsault, Bowser uses meteor strike and Donkey Kong unleashes his DK dash!

Some courses, like Spiky Palms and Bonny Greens, are for beginners. If you want a more challenging game, select Blustery Basin or All-Star Summit. Bowser Highlands was created by the Koopa King to really put Mario in a golfing spin!

Enter golf tournaments to earn winnings and the more experience your golfer has, the higher levels he or she will reach. Spend your earnings on upgrading your stats, with power and running speed two key areas to improve!

TOP TIP!

Pick up course items to boost your stamina!

MARIO & SONIC AT THE OLYMPIC GAMES

With 21 3D sporting events and 10 2D activities, this Olympic festival is a big sporting challenge for Mario and Sonic. Skateboarding, surfing, sport climbing and karate are new to this series – pick your character and start winning the battles!

Special SEGA characters Dr. Eggman, Shadow, Silver and Metal Sonic are fierce competitors. Silver uses special psychokinesis, Shadow has chaos emeralds to diffuse space and time and Metal Sonic is a ruthless robot that can copy all Sonic's powers!

TOP TIP!

There are also story mode scenes from the 1964 Tokyo Olympics!

If real sports are no challenge for you, then let your dreams go wild! *Mario & Sonic at the Olympic Games* also has weird dream events: dream racing, dream karate and dream shooting. Just let your imagination lead you to the gold medal!

MY MARIO GAMES

Write your five favourites. Pick from this selection or any other games you like!

1

2

3

4

5

NINTENDO LEGENDS

As well as the cool characters from the Super Mario world, there are loads more Nintendo gaming greats and legends!

PIKACHU
GAMES: POKÉMON

SPARKS FLYING

There are over 1,000 different Pokémon creatures from Nintendo's amazing Pokémon games, but the top star is definitely Pikachu! First appearing in 1996, this character is an electric elemental class Pokémon, which means it's really buzzed and charged during battles!

POPULAR POKÉMON

With its lightning-bolt shaped tail, smiling face and red cheeks, there's no mistaking Pikachu. From trading card games to adventures on Switch and toy figures, tens of millions of Pikachus exist in the world. *Pokémon Scarlet & Pokémon Violet* sold over ten million copies in the first three days in 2022!

FIGHTING TOUGH

Pikachu has popped up in the Super Smash Bros. series of games. Being quick around the screen and athletic, Pikachu's final smash move is the volt tackle. Stand back as it creates a devastating ball of electricity to inflict on opponents!

SPECIAL DAY

Pokémon Day is celebrated every year on 27 February. The game launched on that date in 1996!

LINK
GAMES: THE LEGEND OF ZELDA

ROYAL PROTECTOR

Always on a quest to protect and battle alongside Princess Zelda, Link is a mighty fighter who uses his master sword and hylian shield for maximum impact! *Link's Awakening, A Link to the Past* and *The Adventure of Link* are great games where he gets to star in the title too!

KART HERO

Look out for Link appearing in *Mario Kart 8*! The Hyrule circuit, based on the Hyrule kingdom from the Zelda games, also shows up. He reaches awesome speeds on the master cycle – equipped with triforce tyres, man and machine are tough to beat!

KIRBY
GAMES: VARIOUS

KIRBY RETURNS

Kirby's Return to *Dreamland Deluxe* came to the Switch in 2023. You and three other players can link up with the bouncy pink hero and journey through Dream Land as you assist Magolor in fixing his crashed aircraft! Kirby first showed up in 1992 and Nintendo fans love his moves.

SPECIAL SKILLS

Described as a puffball, Kirby has slick moves to defeat his opponents. He likes to suck in his foes and other objects and then copy their skills – smart stuff, hey? Imagine being able to inhale a car, which then makes YOU become a car so you can speed off. No other character is quite like Kirby!

KEN MASTERS
GAMES: SUPER SMASH BROS.

MASTER MOVES

Mega martial arts hero Ken Masters made his Nintendo debut in *Street Fighter* on the SNES console, back in 1992. Along with his friend-turned-rival Ryu, American-born Ken can take on the baddest girls and guys in street combat. His special move is the powerful shoryuken!

SMASHING ENTRANCE

The shoryuken is a menacing flying uppercut – avoid it all costs! Ken is a legend in Nintendo's *Super Smash Bros.* series of games. In *Super Smash Bros. Ultimate*, Ken appeared as an echo fighter to Ryu, but with a bit more speed and a special skill in cool combat kicks. His muscles and technique make him so tough to defeat!

INKLINGS
GAMES: SPLATOON

INK-CREDIBLE

Inklings and Octolings are the main players in the *Splatoon* range of games. Called 'squid kids', they can turn from kid to squid in a flash! During play these will blast ink from their weapons as they try to get ink on as many spots as possible and claim the upper hand in turf wars. Take cover!

SPLAT ATTACK

In 2023's *Splatoon 3* game, Splatsville is a chaotic city and the biggest place in the Splatlands region. Inklings can use new ink-splatting tools, like the crab tank and bow-shaped sling shots, to cover their targets and surrounding areas. The Inklings never back down from a colourful clash!

SPECIES SPLAT

Inklings come from the cephalopod species – mysterious underwater creatures that include squid and octopus!

RABBIDS
GAMES: VARIOUS

CHAOTIC CREATURES
You've seen the Rabbids on page 53 and know they're manic creatures! Rabbids debuted in 2006 with the *Rayman Raving Rabbids* game. Since then, their displays in *Rabbids Invasion, Mario + Rabbids Kingdom Battle* and *Mario + Rabbids: Sparks of Hope* have been awesome!

FRANTIC FUN
The Rabbid Luigi character is just like regular Luigi, but with extra bravery to help Rabbid Mario to success! The Rabbids may be one of the weirdest looking species to appear on Nintendo consoles, but start controlling them with your joycon and you'll have plenty of laughs!

SAMUS ARAN
GAMES: METROID

GALACTIC GREAT
Want to be an intergalactic bounty hunter? Load up *Metroid Prime* or *Metroid Dread* on Switch and you will be! Samus Aran has been beating the baddies since the 1980s on the original Nintendo Entertainment System. She's a warrior with epic weapons and fighting skills!

METROID TARGETS
Samus Aran sets her deadly sights on the Metroids. Metroids are a wide range of creepy creatures, created by the powerful Chozo army, that include the jellyfish-like Metroid Larva. Samus also faces a new enemy – the E.M.M.I. robots – during the *Metroid Prime* game!

FOX McCLOUD
GAMES: STAR FOX

SKY HIGH

A Nintendo all-star, this classic character is a high-class pilot and fighter. Fox McCloud is the leader of a fab flying force called the Star Fox team, which also features his allies Falco, Peppy and Slippy. Together they cruise the skies to protect the galaxy from attacks!

MEGA McCLOUD

McCloud's aircraft is the powerful and agile Arwing. The Star Fox team comes up against Andross, the emperor of a planet called Venom, and they need deadly accurate shooting to take him down in space. It's high speed, high altitude adventures all the way with McCloud!

PAC-MAN
GAMES: VARIOUS

HUNGRY HERO

A mega munching machine, Pac-Man has been in over 100 computer games since the 1980s! Pac-Man has a big fear of ghosts, but when he enters a 3D platform puzzle arena he speeds off and jumps, rolls and bounces through stages to reach his target and complete tricky tests!

ACTION & ADVENTURE

Pac-Man has grown from being an arcade hero of the 1980s and '90s to a superstar of Nintendo Switch games! Have a go on the fun 2022 title *Pac-Man World Re-Pac* – it's a crazy mix of quick puzzles, skills, boss battles and loads more. You'll blitz through every mission thanks to Pac-Man's power!

TOP TIP!

Go supersized as MEGA Pac-Man to tower over the enemies!

SONIC
GAMES: VARIOUS

SPEEDY STAR
Sonic, or Sonic the Hedgehog to give him his full name, is one of the biggest ever Nintendo stars! Despite not appearing on Nintendo consoles until 2001, Sonic soon zoomed to become a gaming great. Games like *Sonic Origins*, *Sonic Colours* and *Sonic Frontiers* are huge!

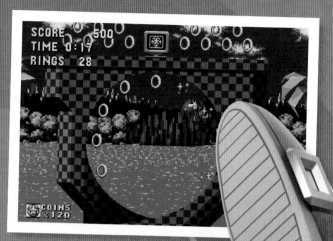

FINAL FRONTIERS
Check out *Sonic Frontiers* on Switch. Explore Starfall Islands as the lightning-fast hero, searching for Chaos Emeralds and looking to avoid the dangers of Cyber Space. Solve challenges and puzzles to unlock entrances, earn vault keys and unleash his new cyloop ability!

FAST MOVES
In the *Sonic Frontiers* game, select the high speed setting if you're a pro at powering Sonic!

TOP POWERS
Sonic's amazing speed is his greatest weapon... blink and he's gone! Over the years he has had plenty of enemies and battles, with Dr. Eggman (also known as Robotnik) being his arch rival. Luckily, Sonic has Tails, Knuckles, Amy and Silver to help him keep the evil Eggman in check.

TOP 10 NINTENDO GAMES

Beyond the Mario universe, plenty of other incredible games have graced Nintendo consoles. Check out some of the top choices!

1 FIFA

SOCCER STARS

FIFA has been around for 30 years! The world's best football game has featured the coolest players, teams, tournaments, stadiums and trophies and no other console experience comes close to beating it. You need slick skills to boss this on Nintendo Switch!

AWESOME EA SPORTS

EA Sports is the company that made FIFA for so long. After *FIFA 23* the game took a new name, but there's no doubt that EA are the legends when it comes to footy powers on a virtual pitch. The HyperMotion 2 technology uses over 6,000 true-to-life animations to make the action look just like the real thing!

WORLD STARS

FIFA has a long history of making World Cup-based football editions that goes back to the 1990s. Seeing Ronaldo, Messi, Kane, Neymar and Mbappe turn on the style for their country and be powered by your fingertips is one of the best feelings a gamer can get!

FANCY FOOTWORK

Dribbling, shooting, passing and free-kicks have all been enhanced and improved in recent years by the FIFA makers. But it's not all made for the attacking team to blast in loads of goals – the clever machine-learning jockey skill lets defenders steal the ball from forwards and launch their own goal raids!

WOMEN'S GAME

FIFA has been a real force in women's football. *FIFA 23* brings together the Women's Super League, UEFA Women's Champions League, National Women's Soccer League and other top-level female events. Seeing on-fire strikers like Sam Kerr and Lauren James smash in goals is a big buzz!

FIFA RANGE

It's not just regular season games that has made FIFA the king of the computer pitch. Updates and new twists over the years, such as *FIFA Street*, *FIFA World* and *FIFA Manager*, have sold millions around the globe. EA Sports keeps coming up with the best ideas and kicks the opposition into second place!

SUPER SKILLS

For the first time, Marvel joined the *FIFA 23* game in a special superhero players' update!

2 LEGO

FAST FACT

Speed through a new location called Bricklander in the 2023 racing game *LEGO 2K Drive!*

BRICK BATTLES

Hundreds of LEGO games and downloads have made their way to Nintendo. From Star Wars to Avengers, Spider-Man, Harry Potter and Ninjago, the bricktastic adventures and heroes are endless.
The 2023 hit *Star Wars: The Skywalker Saga* is the best so far!

HERO STATUS

Marvel and DC content stays mega popular on Nintendo. Load up *Marvel Super Heroes* and control a cool character like Iron Man or Thor against bad dudes such as Venom, Doctor Octopus and Green Goblin. In *DC Super-Villains*, you create your own villains and saviours to lead brave rescue missions!

STAR GAME

Billed as "the biggest Lego videogame yet" by the developers, The *Skywalker Saga* mixes action from nine spectacular Skywalker films. Choosing to start with *The Phantom Menace*, *The Force Awakens* or *A New Hope*, gamers explore galaxies and unlock planets as they fight enemies and solve puzzles and quests!

3 POKÉMON

SPECIAL SERIES

You've read about the powerful Pikachu, and now it's time to explore the glory of the Pokémon series in more detail! The first releases for Nintendo Switch were *Pokémon: Let's Go Pikachu* and *Pokémon: Let's Go Evee. Scarlet & Violet, Brilliant Diamond & Shining Pearl* and *Sword & Shield* have also rocked!

NEW POKÉMON

Do you know of the Pokémon called Sprigatito, Quaxly and Fuecoco? Or what about Koraidon and Miraidon? Pick up the *Scarlet & Violet* editions and you soon will! As the first open-world roleplay games in this series, enjoy new tera raid battles alongside three other Pokémon trainers. Enter Paldea with caution, though!

AUTO ACTION

Enable the auto battle mode and you don't have to do the hard work. Your Pokémon companion will then engage with any other wild Pokémon it finds and collect EXP points and items. Just send it off in any direction, using the 'let's go' feature. Relax and enjoy.

4

THE LEGEND OF ZELDA

TOP TEARS

There was a lot of excitement around the 2023 release of the new *Tears of the Kingdom* game, the latest instalment in the Zelda series. Following *Breath of the Wild*, *Link's Awakening* and *Skyward Sword* on the Switch console, Zelda fans ordered the latest version very quickly!

FLASHBACK

Want to go Zelda retro? Get the classic *Legend of Zelda* game on the little Game & Watch device!

SKY ADVENTURE

This time, the action reaches the skies as well as the land as Link explores the mysterious Hyrule. There are new vehicles and weapons, plus huge new abilities for our hero to unleash. Check out the floating islands and leave no stone unturned as you take down opponents in style!

LINK UP

Tears of the Kingdom on Switch gave Link some interesting new powers, like ultrahand and fuse to allow him to make epic new weapons. The new ascend ability allows him to pass through objects, hillsides, ceilings and even some enemies. These shortcuts can be such a boost!

5 ANIMAL CROSSING

ANIMAL ADVENTURE

Animal Crossing goes back to 2004, when it appeared on the Nintendo GameCube. The sim-based game came exclusively to Switch in 2020 when *Animal Crossing: New Horizons* launched on the system. With Tom Nook as your guide, build your own island, meet neighbours and have a fun time!

ISLAND LIFE

New Horizons gives you the chance to explore a dream new island and totally relax in gaming paradise. Use your new NookPhone, with its apps, camera and maps, to create things around you and complete challenges to earn Nook Miles rewards. Updates always keep *Animal Crossing* fun and there's always a reason to visit!

6 NINTENDO SWITCH SPORTS

SPORTS SHOW

Wii Sports was a huge hit for Nintendo in 2006 as friends and families played tennis, golf, tenpin bowling and all sorts of activities on the Wii. When *Switch Sports* came to the Switch system in 2022, it took home gaming experiences to the next level!

GAME ON

Football, badminton, volleyball and foam swordplay were added events for *Switch Sports*. Use the JoyCon controller and the leg strap device to really kick off your sporty quests. Take on a friend, customize your sportsmate avatar and see if you can reach pro status on the sports field!

TOP 10
NINTENDO GAMES

7 HOGWARTS LEGACY

MAGICAL MISSION

The Lego Harry Potter games are epic, but 2023's *Hogwarts Legacy* on Switch takes the magical action to another level! Gamers take centre stage in their own wizarding world, leading an adventure as a student at the legendary Hogwarts School in the 1800s. It's slick and stylish.

WIZARD WAYS

Take on dark wizards, craft helpful potions, create engaging spells and raise your skills to become the wizard with the best powers. *Hogwarts Legacy* sold millions of copies in the first few weeks as Harry Potter fans rushed to explore this fascinating world!

8 MINECRAFT LEGENDS

LEGENDS ENTER

Minecraft finally arrived on Nintendo when the Switch came out in 2017. *Minecraft Legends* is the latest twist in this mighty series, following after *Minecraft Dungeons*. A full-on action strategy experience, lead your friends and heroes in the Overworld and beat the powerful piglin enemies!

OVERWORLD BATTLE

You must stop the Nether corruption from taking control of the Overworld. With villagers, zombies and llamas everywhere, face the Piglins and raid their bases without fear, making sure your strategy for day and night raids are well carried out. It's like the Minecraft you know and love, but with so much added excitement!

9 | SPONGEBOB

UNDERWATER ADVENTURES

The Spongebob platform and puzzle games for Nintendo have some of the wackiest names ever, such as *Battle for Bikini Bottom*, *Krusty Cook-Off* and the *Cosmic Shake*. The oceanic hero is always teaming up with his pals Patrick, Squidward, Mr. Krabs and Sandy to stop the evil plans of Plankton!

COSMIC CRUSADE

The *Cosmic Shake* came to Switch in 2023. Here, Spongebob and Balloon Patrick visit seven fun worlds, including Wild West Jellyfish Fields and Halloween Rock Bottom. With cowboys, knights and prehistoric snails roaming, the gang can unlock new and classic moves and use over 30 crazy costumes. Bikini Bottom is ready for fun!

10 | JUST DANCE

GAME GROOVE

All gamers like action, quests, battles and problem solving, but having a cheeky dance is always fun too! The popular *Just Dance* games have been great, going back to the original Wii years ago. On Switch, these titles are such a laugh as friends and families copy the coolest dance moves on screen.

POP STARS

Dance and groove to the greatest tunes from artists like Harry Styles, Imagine Dragons, Billie Eilish, Zara Larsson and BTS. *Just Dance 2023* has a new progression system, based on how well you synch to the instructions displayed. Plus, the app makes your smartphone a cool controller with phone-scoring tech. Bust the best moves!

WORD SEARCH

Track down all these Nintendo heroes and games in the grid!

M	B	C	R	Y	F	F	Z	X	W	S	G	G	O	X	Z	P
P	K	U	P	S	I	N	N	E	T	O	I	R	A	M	E	I
S	U	P	E	R	M	A	R	I	O	3	D	W	O	R	L	D
F	A	P	P	L	U	Z	H	D	O	S	Z	P	R	I	D	S
C	G	P	S	V	Y	M	B	Z	P	R	R	E	W	J	A	R
G	H	C	O	J	F	Z	V	O	E	I	K	Q	Q	C	E	E
J	Z	S	N	A	O	R	N	V	N	B	I	K	Q	M	I	T
E	Q	D	I	E	L	G	A	C	M	K	R	M	N	P	J	S
P	R	S	C	R	E	I	E	W	E	S	B	I	C	I	K	A
L	I	Y	P	B	T	S	Y	M	E	N	Y	I	K	K	L	M
V	K	K	O	L	S	T	R	A	K	O	I	R	A	M	J	N
P	H	B	A	P	A	D	O	I	E	V	M	L	D	X	R	E
P	A	Y	E	C	N	T	Z	Z	I	Y	Q	K	U	M	T	K
R	U	A	V	Q	H	G	O	S	Y	E	R	R	V	A	R	A
V	C	D	J	U	C	U	C	O	W	Z	F	B	T	H	P	Q
H	M	I	I	G	R	Y	V	P	N	X	N	K	G	R	K	J
H	V	I	D	I	D	D	Y	K	O	N	G	D	A	X	V	J

SUPER MARIO 3D WORLD   **MARIO KART**   **PRINCESS PEACH**   **KIRBY**

ZELDA   **MARIO TENNIS**   **KEN MASTERS**   **SONIC**   **PAULINE**   **LINK**

DIDDY KONG   **SPLATOON**   **PIKACHU**   **SPONGEBOB**   **CAPPY**

ANSWERS ON PAGE 78

MISSING LETTERS

Read the six clues, then write the answer for each. You will reveal a mystery character in the middle!

1 ▢▢▢▢ - ▢▢▢▢

2 ▢▢▢▢▢▢▢▢▢▢▢▢

3 ▢▢▢▢▢▢▢

4 ▢▢▢▢▢▢▢▢

5 ▢▢▢▢▢▢▢▢▢

6 ▢▢▢▢▢

1 Mario's most explosive enemy.

2 This creature has the nickname 'DK'.

3 Has an upside down 'L' on his cap.

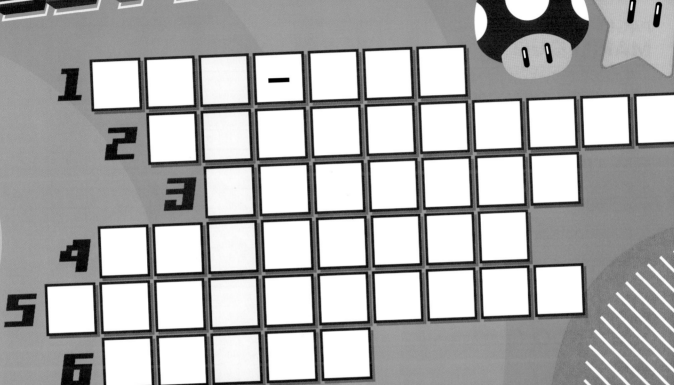

4 A princess, but not Peach.

5  MARIO PARTY

In the name of a cool Mario Party game.

6 The number one hero in the Mushroom Kingdom!

THE MYSTERY CHARACTER IS: ....

ANSWERS ON PAGE 78

ANSWERS

PAGES 26–27
MARIO QUIZ

1. B - Jumpman
2. C - Mushroom Kingdom
3. B - 1981
4. A - Super Mario Smash
5. A - A Painting
6. C - March 10
7. A - 2008
8. B - Mario Kart 8 Deluxe
9. A - Brothers
10. C - Yoshi

PAGES 50 – 51
NINTENDO QUIZ

1. Bowser
2. Japan
3. Boo
4. Wario
5. Tetris
6. Koopalings
7. Goombas
8. Super Nintendo Entertainment System
9. 2017
10. Crocodile

PAGE 76
WORDSEARCH

PAGE 77
MISSING LETTERS

BO**B**-OMB
DONKEYKONG
WALUIGI
R**O**SALINA
SUP**E**RSTARS
MA**R**IO